"If an approach is elegant
it may be getting near
to what's true."

Henri Cartier-Bresson

Published by the Lehigh University Alumni Association
& Harmony House Publishers (502)-228-2010

Being Lehigh Book copyright 1996 Lehigh University
Alumni Association

Second Edition printed Fall 1997

Foreword by Don Bott '54, Executive Director Emeritus
copyright 1996 Lehigh University Alumni Association

Afterword by Marvin Simmons
copyright 1996 Lehigh University

Henri Cartier-Bresson quote copyright Henri
Cartier-Bresson interviewed by John Berger from
On Location: Six Portfolios, Aperture, New York 1995.
Used by permission.

Being Lehigh Photographs, Design, & Copy
copyright 1996 H. Scott Heist

ISBN–1–56469-030-x Library of Congress–96-076276
Printed in Canada

Typography and production assistance
by Saraceno Design Inc., Bethlehem, Pennsylvania

On a warm Indian Summer day in the mid-1950s, my dad held my hand and we walked up the stone steps to Linderman Library. They were large and Dad had to lift me step to step but, only after I tried each one and we were both certain I couldn't make it on my own. The doors were too heavy for me to manage. The floor was hard and cold. I slipped on it quite a few times. The underside of the card catalog table was finished in the same color as the top. Yellow light skated on hand polished surfaces.

Dad was finishing his grad work. I could come along to the library "so long as I treated it as a church." And the books, in the long, never-ending stacks were the source of this reverence. "Learn to put your thoughts down on paper." That was the litany Dad whispered to me from the wooden study chairs pointing to all the stacks on all the floors.

Later, I sat with Mum at Dad's graduation. In those days, graduations went on for untold hours and important men in black robes spoke until you fell asleep on your mother's shoulder. Afterwards we all hugged, and today, still, graduations for me smell of Arpege and Old Spice. And the bright smiles bring yellow sunshine. For education was something the whole family achieved together. And would share.

Many, many summers later, I walked my son Chris up those same stairs, holding his hand and lifting him where necessary. Marvin Simmon's office at Publications was on the top floor of Linderman Library. There I could share with Chris what I had learned. On the shelves are the efforts of Mr. Shakespeare, Mr. Camus, Mr. Cartier-Bresson and thousands of others. Including your grandfather. In these books the thoughts of others are waiting. And if you enter their pages with an open mind, they contain the magic to change your life. Each time you read them. Hopefully, this volume enters the circle.

So my efforts here are dedicated to the heroes of my life, Evelyn and Horace Heist, who with strong hand and gentle heart, started me on my journey. And of course, to Chris, who continues to share it and add so much to it.

To all about to embark on such a journey, we wish Godspeed.

H. Scott Heist
Splinter Cottage

being
Lehigh

an essay in photographs
by
H. Scott Heist
and
a foreword:
the magic and memories
by
Don Bott '54
an afterword: a vision
by
Marvin Simmons

being

Lehigh

an essay in photographs
by
H. Scott Heist
and
a foreword:
the magic and memories
by
Don Bott, '54
an afterword: a vision
by
Marvin Simmons

Contents:

Dedication 6

Foreword
 by Don Bott '54 9

Beginning
 by H. Scott Heist 11

Arriving 20

Reading 30

Listening 38

Living
 by H. Scott Heist 55

Thinking 62

Holding 75

Cheering 81

Flying 89

Walking 95

Understanding 103

Returning
 by H. Scott Heist 115

Afterword
 by Marvin Simmons 129

Notes & Sources 131

The magic and memories:

a foreword   by Don Bott '54

For the last nineteen years Scott Heist has been the photojournalist who captured the magic of our Lehigh University with his eye, his camera, his magnificent photographs. We have all looked at and rejoiced in his art as it distinguished itself in receiving more than thirty awards for his work in our *Lehigh Alumni Bulletin*. Over the years, he has shown us with his honest, unposed photography, the smiles and enthusiasm of our Lehigh family members as well as the gothic beauty of Lehigh's architecture. All this amidst the nature preserve that we have been privileged to share on South Mountain.

This collection provides a visual history of our Lehigh of the '80s and '90s. Imagine a distant relative visiting the campus one hundred years from now, looking up at the gargoyles on the Packer Chapel tower or at the faces carved in stone on the portals of the Alumni Memorial Building. Will they still be there? Will there still be the exhilarated smiles of young men and women undergraduates as they discover, accomplish, and experience a first-time event in their young lives?

Take time to study the photographs and the many expressions of joy. This joy is also with our older alumni as we view their savoring of the days of yore. Their eyes have a knowing smile and we reflect with them in Scott's photographs.

In **Being Lehigh**, we have a beautiful history that will be viewed by our 22nd century legacies, the future Lehigh family members. We'll probably look rather different because of our clothes and hairstyles. I would wager that one hundred years from now people will comment about that fellow, Heist, and his timeless wonderful photographs. As his friend, and as a provider of feedback from alumni and friends, I thank Scott Heist for his superb visual gifts in the *Lehigh Alumni Bulletin* and for this collection. You, the viewer and reader, we thank for being an important part of this experience. For **Being Lehigh**.

The magic and memories:

a foreword

For the last nineteen years Scott Heist
the magic of our Lehigh University
photographs. We have all looked
itself in receiving more than
Lehigh Alumni Bulletin.
with his honest, unposed
and enthusiasm of our
as well as the gothic beauty
All this amidst the nature
been privileged to share

This collection
Lehigh of the '80s
relative visiting the campus
now, looking up at the gargoyles
tower or at the faces carved
the Alumni Memorial Building. Will they
exhilarated smiles of young men and women
accomplish, and experience a first-time event in their young lives?

Take time to study the photographs and the many expressions of joy. This joy is also with our older alumni as we view their savoring of the days of yore. Their eyes have a knowing smile and we reflect with them in Scott's photographs.

In Being Lehigh, we have a beautiful history that will be viewed by our 22nd century legacies, the future Lehigh family members. We'll probably look rather different because of our clothes and hairstyles. I would wager that one hundred years from now people will comment about that fellow, Heist, and his timeless wonderful photographs. As his friend, and as a provider of feedback from alumni and friends, I thank Scott Heist for his superb visual gifts in the Lehigh Alumni Bulletin and for this collection. You, the viewer and reader, we thank for being an important part of this experience. For Being Lehigh.

by Don Bott, '54

has been the photojournalist who captured
with his eye, his camera, his magnificent
art and rejoiced in his art as it distinguished
thirty awards for his work in our
Over the years, he has shown us
photography, the smiles
Lehigh family members
of Lehigh's architecture.
preserve that we have
on South Mountain.

provides a visual history of our
and '90s. Imagine a distant
one hundred years from
on the Packer Chapel
in stone on the portals of
still be there? Will there still be the
undergraduates as they discover,

Beginning

Where the Lehigh's rocky rapids rush from out the west,
Mid a grove of spreading chestnuts, walls in ivy dressed,
On the breast of old South Mountain, reared against the sky,
Stands our noble Alma Mater, stands our dear Lehigh.

The Lehigh River flows through the valley. Above the river in the mountain's sides were the resources upon which Asa Packer built his fortune. Beside the river on the canals and tracks, lay the means. Asa built his home into the side of the mountain. Through recessed windows came the yellow autumns and the green springs. Asa could see the Lehigh River and his dreams flowing together. He seemed to like mountainsides.

Asa had Lehigh built of hand-cut rock into the side of another mountain. Thirty miles south of his home. With the hands of Italian craftsmen, marble was cut for the baptistry in his daughter Mary's chapel. With the eye of Louis Comfort Tiffany, the glass of the chapel's mural was stained ruby red. Lehigh was built to last, of stone and buttress, like the great learning centers of Europe. Its tall stone towers designed to be seen against the sky. To inspire and create respect. To demonstrate the power of possibility. The concept of a man who made his own journey to Pennsylvania on foot and learned to appreciate the power of a mountainside.

And not far away, in stone classrooms, young men sat on wooden chairs before slate blackboards trimmed in a similar wood, beginning a solid tradition which would bring all races, faiths, and both sexes to the side of the mountain. To walk the path up the hill, where we would all learn from each other to be Lehigh.

arriving

reading

listening

Living

Like a watchman on the mountain, stands she grandly bold,
Earth's and Heaven's secrets seeking, hoarding them like gold.
All she wrests from nature's storehouse, naught escapes her eye,
Gives she gladly to her dear ones, while we bless Lehigh.

It is a gentle winter day in the early '80s. We are working on the University Annual Report featuring graduating seniors. Lori Roth '84 is walking with us. Through the grove below Alumni Memorial and beside Packard Lab, where the leaves have given way to winter and the trees stand no straighter than they have to. It's quiet and peaceful. The slope of the pathway is gentle. Perhaps the only place on the old campus where one can walk uphill without conscious effort. Lori recounts her first visit. What her mother said after walking out of the doors of Alumni onto the old campus. "Oh, it's just like a movie. You're going here." The decision was made. Lori tells the story with a smile.

The grove is an open space. Place for the leaves and squirrels and a little breathing room. A place for echoes of hard work to die down to the silence of calm. A place where the lessons get fixed. Legend has it that once there were thoughts of putting the business school here. It was empty and therefore setting on the first ledge of availability. But an alumnus benefactor thought differently. That the campus was right the way it was and provided expansion land on the other side of the mountain which became the Goodman Campus. And the leaves and squirrels and class after class of students continue to have that breathing room. Just like the generations before them. To walk through and remember for the rest of their lives. An example of another kind of building.

All the seasons' colors live there. It is most striking in the morning sun. In the autumn, sound carries, working its way downhill through the stone buildings to what has now come to be known, tongue a little to cheek, as "the sacred grove". A call from a friend. The voice young and robust. A bit of organ music from the chapel. The singing of a bird. The crackle of the blowing leaves. The din of life's promise.

So, perhaps twenty years later in the midst of a stressful day, it comes back. Arriving like an unexpected friend. Just for a moment and a smile. The sacred grove was never empty. It is where the memories are stored.

<u>thinking</u>

73

holding

cheering

85

flying

walking

understanding

105

Returning

We will ever live to love her, live to praise her name;
Live to make our lives add luster to her glorious fame.
Let the glad notes wake the echo, joyfully we cry,
Hail to thee, our Alma Mater! Hail, all Hail Lehigh!

Bill Weeks '39 is sitting in the Cafe Mozart on the Avenue Mozart in Paris. It is August of 1995. The light is soft and timeless. He is a former publisher of the *Paris Herald Tribune*, an author and a partner in one of the respected career counseling firms of Europe. He is speaking about his time at Lehigh: "One of my finest memories is of lying on the grass next to Packer Chapel listening to the Bach Choir. The best years of my life. I really enjoyed it." Les Whitten '50 lives near Washington where he wrote a syndicated column with Jack Anderson. Now he writes novels and translates poems. He is looking wistfully at a photograph of the sun making its way along the road below Linderman Library. "That's just the way it looked the day I arrived." He is smiling, shoulders relaxed. "Lehigh taught me to say yes to life."

And then, twenty-five years later ... "my first memory is of one of those cool, cloudy, Bethlehem days. My parents and I parked below the University Center and I knew this was the school I wanted to attend. It felt like home, but also, a new beginning." Phyllis Errico '81, an attorney, speaks from her home in Virginia. "The campus embraces you and the people do as well. The personal connection made my parents feel at ease. When we left, returning home to Massachusetts, our questions had been answered. We all knew I was going to Lehigh and that it was the right decision. It is a feeling that has never left me. Now that I am a Lehigh trustee, I come back a great deal. Each time I return, I feel renewed."

The story repeats. But is not repetitive. With alumni of all sorts. The aesthetics of the old campus combines with the memories of a few friends, teachers, and classmates. A warm day, a yellow leaf, a thought never experienced before, a laugh shared. All of which made a small but indelible difference. Those who took a few special experiences in a few short years and made them a philosophy. Who made life an adventure by understanding what learning really is. Not one thing but the combination of many. A way of looking at life perhaps. The ability to choose and make sound judgments. To know the difference between complexity and confusion. Between patina and peeling paint. To know what is old and may need to be replaced. And what is old, strong, and should be shared. In the sharing, the thinking, the believing and the dreaming, the being of Lehigh continues. To change while remaining the same. And there, the mystery becomes the magic.

an afterword
by Marvin Simmons
Director of Design,
Lehigh University

A Vision

In a time

where and when

expediency can swallow experience,

it is refreshing to see the world through a real observer's eyes.

I remember working on a painting when for the first time, I began

really to see an environment. It was almost as if a small veil of superficiality

had been removed. It is no less important in photography. Here it may mean waiting

for human nature to define the decisive moment and motion to be captured, making it

possible to see again. Documenting, yes, but also eliciting a subject's response, completing

the triad of subject, photographer, and viewer. Cartier-Bresson shares the reality of his vision

through black and white prints that elicit an emotion beyond time and place. Scott Heist has

preserved for us, much of it in color, those universal expressions that touch us now,

as when first seen. How unusual that a vision occurs, from commercial publications, that

is often more honest than flattering. Lehigh is enriched by a body of work that is rare.

If found at all, it is in the personal vision of the artist.

an afterword
by Marvin Simmons
Director of Design,
Lehigh University

A Vision

In a time

where and when

expediency can swallow experience,

it is refreshing to see the world through a real observer's eyes.

I remember working on a painting when for the first time, I began

really to see an environment. It was almost as if a small veil of superficiality

had been removed. It is no less important in photography. Here it may mean waiting

for human nature to define the decisive moment and motion to be captured, making it

possible to see again. Documenting, yes, but also eliciting a subject's response, completing

the triad of subject, photographer, and viewer. Cartier-Bresson shares the reality of his vision

through black and white prints that elicit an emotion beyond time and place. Scott Heist has

preserved for us, much of it in color, those universal expressions that touch us now,

as when first seen. How unusual that a vision occurs, from commercial publications, that

is often more honest than flattering. Lehigh is enriched by a body of work that is rare.

If found at all, it is in the personal vision of the artist.

Notes & Sources .... as per best recollection

Cover: Oct. '88, midday, recruitment cover, poster, postcard ... this was my birthday and another 8 photos in the book came to us that day. Never was the light so handsome and the film so good. A true gift. End pieces: women's rowing team Oct. '93, 5:00 a.m., recruitment, unused. 2-3: Another from the 1988 Birthday shoot, magazine article. 4-5: May '92, for First USA Bank for a Lehigh Visa Card I was designing. We used the more conservative image still in use. Later used in recruitment. 6: May '94, tulip found outside the Alumni building, recruitment. 7: May '94, again the Alumni building, recruitment cover, poster, postcard. 8: Nov. '93, Goodman Stadium, Alumni weekend, magazine. 9: June '94, Linderman Library gargoyle, magazine cover. 10: June '83, Asa Packer's cane, made from a deer spine, and chair at the Packer Mansion, magazine cover, a number of awards. 12-13: June '83, Packer family photographs as found in bedroom of Packer home, magazine essay. 14-15&16: June '87, a magazine story on the 100th year of Packer Church. 17,18,19: April '90, Packard Labs classroom, recruitment, magazine, posters. 20-21: Aug. '89, from the *Colors of a University* recruitment brochure which won lots of awards. 22-23: May '95, flagpole area Packer Campus, recruitment. 24: Aug. '92, a magazine article on the first day, recruitment. 25: June '95, packing to leave on upper campus, recruitment. 26: Sept. '92, first day article for magazine cover. 26-27: Aug. '89, arriving, recruitment brochure. 28,29: Aug. '95, arriving at the Packer Church for convocation, magazine. 30: Sept. '90, Linderman Library, magazine cover. 31: Dec.'92, Packard Labs, magazine, recruitment. 32: May '92, studying for finals, Fairchild-Martindale Library lawn, recruitment. 34: May '92, freshmen quad residence halls, recruitment. 35: Nov. '94, Centennial residences, magazine story on student rooms. 36: Feb.'90, Linderman Library, double magazine spread from story on libraries. 37: Aug. '92, Fairchild-Martindale Library, development, *Preserving The Vision* brochure. 38: Oct. '93, Art Studio, Chandler-Ullmann, recruitment. 40: April '88, as above. 41: Oct. '93, music room Lamberton Hall, magazine. 42-43: Nov. '93, an alumnus returns to a class at Rauch Business Center, magazine. 44: Dec. '93, class at the College of Business and Economics, recruitment. 45: April '94, class at the College of Arts & Science, recruitment. 46-47: May '94, radio wave receiver for The World View Room at Maginnes reflected in Fairchild-Martindale Library, recruitment. 48&49: Nov. '95, Packer Church and Alumni Memorial twin spires, recruitment. 50&51: Oct. '88, Goodman Campus, another from the birthday shoot mentioned earlier, recruitment. 52&53: May '95 between Linderman Library and University Center, recruitment. 54: Nov. '94, between Packard Labs and the sacred grove, recruitment, postcards. 56: Dec. '85, the President's home for a holiday card. 57: Feb. '93, Main Campus in the dreaded winter of '93. Later blitzed by '94, magazine. 58-59: Feb. '88, the sacred grove, recruitment. 60-61: February '88, Alumni Memorial at sunset, recruitment. 62: Dec. '88, Alumni Memorial, early morning, recruitment. 63: April '82, this one's a screwball. One of my favorites, and believe it or not, one of the most used photographs at Lehigh. Snow came in April and I went to photograph it on the magnolias. This gentleman and I played hide and seek behind the hedges. When I stopped to do some work, he wondered what the problem was. That day the snow and ice blew two cameras. I worked at a loss and if I had the chance to do it again...in a minute, magazine cover, recruitment pieces (3), postcards. 64: June '94, detail Linderman Library, reunion magazine. 65: May '94, finals, Fairchild-Martindale Library. 66: May '92, Mountaintop Campus, Iacocca Building, recruitment. 67: April '87, baptistery, Packer Church, recruitment. 68-69: April '88, origami engineering project, brochure for the opening of Mohler Labs, magazine. 70: Feb. '93, Linderman Library at exam time, magazine. 71: April '94, architectural project main campus, recruitment. 72-73: Jan. '93, architectural project in lobby Iacocca Hall, recruitment, magazine. Also a special spread in *The Chronicle of Higher Education*. 74: Feb. '95, wrestling at Stabler Center, magazine. 75: Oct. '93, reflection of rower in Lehigh River, magazine. 76: April '93, Goodman Field, magazine. 77: April '91, intramural soccer at Goodman Field, recruitment. 78-79: Nov. '93, Goodman field, magazine. 80: '82, Taylor Stadium, recruitment, magazine. 81: Oct. '91, cheering Czech President Havel at Stabler Center, magazine. 82-83: June '92, graduation at Stabler Center, magazine. 84: June '94, graduation Goodman Campus, recruitment. 85: Oct. '91, Goodman Field, magazine. 86-87: June 88, graduation in front of Rauch Field House, recruitment, magazine. 88: Nov. '81, Alumni Memorial, recruitment. 89: April '93, women's baseball, Goodman Campus, recruitment. 90: Nov. '81, Taylor Stadium, recruitment. 91: Feb. '94, Taylor Gym, magazine. 92-93: Sept. '89, first day freshman quad, cover recruitment brochure. 94: Sept. '82, Main Campus for recruitment. 95: Oct.'88, another from the Birthday shoot, toward Packer Church, recruitment. 96: May '94, beside Mart Library, recruitment. 97: Nov. '88, Main Campus, minority recruitment. 98: Sept. '93, Linderman Library, recruitment, postcard. 99: May '90, bus stop at Mart Library, magazine. 100: May '95, Rauch Business Center, recruitment. 101: June '95, graduation, Goodman Stadium. 102: Feb. '95, Boston, magazine alumni story. 103: Nov. '93, Goodman Field, magazine. 104: April '91, Art Studio, Chandler-Ullmann, recruitment. 105: April '94, Packard Labs, student-built race car, recruitment. 106: Sept. '94, bridge testing at ATLSS/Imbt Labs, Mountaintop Campus, magazine. 107: May '93, Civil Engineering students near powerhouse, recruitment. 108: Nov. '89, helicopter above Goodman Stadium in bad weather. We had trouble crossing the mountain, magazine cover. 109: Sept. '81, film test at Goodman Field. 110,111,112&113: Oct. '88, Alumni Memorial, four more from the birthday shoot, magazine, recruitment, posters. 114: June '93, a very wet reunion, magazine cover. 116: Nov. '93, Goodman Stadium, magazine, recruitment. 117: Nov. '90, Goodman Stadium, the coldest, wettest, football game die-hards ever played at or in, magazine cover. 118: June '95, reunion cover...The Bad Boys of June. 119: June '84, reunion friends with dinks, magazine. 120-121: Oct. '91, Goodman Stadium, magazine. 122: May '95, birch near flagpole, recruitment. 123: Jan. '88, Packer Church door, holiday season, used for holiday card. 124: Nov. '86, Linderman Library from a beautiful recruitment piece called *Windows on Your Future*. 125: June '95, Linderman Library door, recruitment, postcard. 126-127: Sept. '90, University Center, recruitment. 128: March '94, Alumni Memorial rear entrance, magazine. 129: July '95, rotunda. Linderman Library, a film test. 130: Aug. '87, magazine cover on Packer Church. 131: Nov. '95, Mountain Hawk Mascot arrives, magazine. Rear cover: Oct. '88, last shot of the day on the birthday shoot, Linderman Library's door almost never closes. 132: June '96, rotunda. Linderman Library recruitment.